D1128455

EXTREME WEATHER

Tornadoes

by Anne Wendorff

Consultant:
Mark Seeley, Ph.D.,
University of Minnesota Extension
Meteorologist and Climatologist,
Department of Soil, Water, and Climate,
St Paul, Minn.

BELLWETHER MEDIA • MINNEAPOLIS, MN

Note to Librarians, Teachers, and Parents:

Blastoff! Readers are carefully developed by literacy experts and combine standards-based content with developmentally appropriate text.

Level 1 provides the most support through repetition of high-frequency words, light text, predictable sentence patterns, and strong visual support.

Level 2 offers early readers a bit more challenge through varied simple sentences, increased text load, and less repetition of high-frequency words.

Level 3 advances early-fluent readers toward fluency through increased text and concept load, less reliance on visuals, longer sentences, and more literary language.

Level 4 builds reading stamina by providing more text per page, increased use of punctuation, greater variation in sentence patterns, and increasingly challenging vocabulary.

Level 5 encourages children to move from "learning to read" to "reading to learn" by providing even more text, varied writing styles, and less familiar topics.

Whichever book is right for your reader, Blastoff! Readers are the perfect books to build confidence and encourage a love of reading that will last a lifetime!

This edition first published in 2009 by Bellwether Media.

No part of this publication may be reproduced in whole or in part without written permission of the publisher. For information regarding permission, write to Bellwether Media Inc., Attention: Permissions Department, Post Office Box 19349, Minneapolis, MN 55419.

Library of Congress Cataloging-in-Publication Data
Wendorff, Anne.
  Tornadoes / by Anne Wendorff.
    p. cm. – (Blastoff! readers. Extreme weather)
  Summary: "Simple text and full color photographs introduce beginning readers to the characteristics of tornadoes. Developed by literacy experts for students in kindergarten through third grade"—Provided by publisher.
  Includes bibliographical references and index.
  ISBN-13: 978-1-60014-187-4 (hardcover : alk. paper)
  ISBN-10: 1-60014-187-0 (hardcover : alk. paper)
  1. Tornadoes—Juvenile literature. I. Title.

QC955.2.W46 2009
551.55'3—dc22   2008015220

Contents

What Is a Tornado?   4

How Do Tornadoes Form?   6

How Tornadoes Look and Behave   10

Predicting Tornadoes   16

Staying Safe in a Tornado   18

Glossary   22

To Learn More   23

Index   24

What Is a Tornado?

Tornadoes are powerful, spinning windstorms that reach from the clouds to the ground.

These wild storms are sometimes called twisters because of their spinning winds.

5

How Do Tornadoes Form?

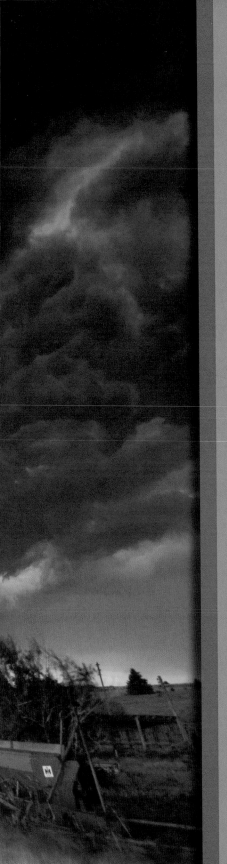

Most tornadoes start in **thunderclouds**. Thunderclouds need certain conditions to form. They need a layer of warm, **moist** air near the ground. They also need a layer of cool air above the warm, moist air.

Warm air rises. It cools as it rises. Cool air cannot hold as much moisture as warm air. The moisture gets squeezed out of the air, like water squeezed out of a sponge. The moisture turns into water droplets floating in clouds. These droplets can build up to form tall, dark thunderclouds.

Inside some thunderclouds, warm air begins rising extremely fast. It also begins moving in a spiral as it rises. This is called an **updraft**.

Sometimes a **funnel cloud** develops at the bottom of a thundercloud, underneath an updraft. This is the beginning of a tornado. A funnel cloud becomes a tornado if it extends and touches the ground.

Not all thunderclouds with updrafts start funnel clouds and not all funnel clouds extend to touch the ground. Scientists aren't certain why these conditions sometimes create tornadoes and sometimes do not.

thundercloud

updraft

funnel cloud

fast fact

Tornadoes can occur anywhere. However, most happen in the American Midwest. The area from north Texas through Oklahoma, Kansas, and Nebraska is sometimes called Tornado Alley.

How Tornadoes Look and Behave

Tornadoes can have different shapes. Some look like long ropes. Others look like wedges.

Some look like giant black clouds. These tornadoes can be very wide. The shape of a tornado does not tell the strength of its winds. Tornadoes of any shape can have powerful winds. Scientists think that the most extreme tornado winds blow at around 300 miles (480 kilometers) per hour. This is faster than wind blows in any other kind of storm.

fast fact

Scientists think that an EF-5 tornado has winds moving at more than 200 miles (322 kilometers) per hour. However, this is a guess because it is difficult to actually measure the wind speed in a tornado.

Fierce winds make it difficult to measure tornadoes while they are happening. Scientists try to measure tornadoes after they are gone by looking at the damage they caused. This is called the **Enhanced Fujita Scale**, or **EF-Scale**.

There are five categories in the EF-Scale. An EF-1 tornado breaks tree branches and causes slight damage to buildings. An EF-5 tornado can lift entire houses off the ground.

A tornado acts like a giant
vacuum cleaner. It sucks up
dirt and loose material from
the ground. These swirl with
the wind. They can make
a tornado appear grey,
brown, or black.

Predicting Tornadoes

Meteorologists watch for tornadoes. They look for updrafts forming in thunderclouds. They announce a **tornado watch** when the weather conditions are right for a tornado. They announce a **tornado warning** when a funnel cloud is spotted.

Staying Safe in a Tornado

In many places, **tornado sirens** will sound when there is a tornado warning. Sirens warn people to prepare for a tornado.

If they hear a siren, people should move to the basement of a sturdy building or to a room with no windows. That keeps them safe from objects that the tornado hurls through the air.

Some tornadoes last only seconds. Some last more than an hour. Most last less than 10 minutes and are on the ground for less than 10 miles (16 kilometers).

Tornadoes eventually lose energy and die out. There is always a lot to clean up after a tornado. People can spend months cleaning up from these powerful twisters.

Glossary

Enhanced Fujita Scale or **EF-Scale**—a scale used to measure the level of damage caused by a tornado; the scale ranges from EF-1 to EF-5.

funnel cloud—a cloud that hangs down from the bottom of a thundercloud and contains spinning winds; a funnel cloud may become a tornado.

meteorologists—scientists who study weather

moist—wet; moist air contains a lot of water in an invisible gas form.

thunderclouds—tall, dark clouds that contain a lot of moisture

tornado sirens—loud warning systems that let people know a tornado may be in the area

tornado warning—a warning issued by the National Weather Service when a tornado is spotted

tornado watch—a warning issued by the National Weather Service when weather conditions could create a tornado

updraft—warm air that is moving upward

To Learn More

AT THE LIBRARY
Berger, Melvin and Gilda. *Do Tornadoes Really Twist? Questions and Answers about Tornadoes and Hurricanes*. New York: Scolastic Inc, 2000.

Katz, Jill. *Tornadoes*. Mankato, Minn.: Smart Apple Media, 2002.

Simon, Seymour. *Tornadoes*. New York: Harper Trophy, 2001.

ON THE WEB
Learning more about the tornadoes is as easy as 1, 2, 3.

1. Go to www.factsurfer.com

2. Enter "tornadoes" into search box.

3. Click the "Surf" button and you will see a list of related web sites.

With factsurfer.com, finding more information is just a click away.

Index

American Midwest, 9
Enhanced Fujita Scale, 12, 13
flying objects, 19
funnel cloud, 8, 9, 16
Kansas, 9
meteorologists, 16
Nebraska, 9
Oklahoma, 9
scientists, 8, 11, 12
Texas, 9
thunderclouds, 7, 8, 9, 16
Tornado Alley, 9
tornado shapes, 10, 11
tornado sirens, 18, 19
tornado warning, 16, 18
tornado watch, 16
updraft, 8, 9, 16
water droplets, 7
waterspout, 15
wind, 5, 11, 12, 15

The images in this book are reproduced through the courtesy of: A. T. Willett / Alamy, front cover, p.12;
Corbis Premium RF / Alamy, p.4; Juan Martinez, pp. 5, 18; Ryan McGinnis / Alamy, p. 6; Linda Clavel,
p. 9; Sean Martin, p. 10; National Geographic / Getty Images, p. 13; Geckophoto, p. 14; Getty Images,
pp. 15, 21; Jim Reed / Getty Images, pp. 16, 17, 19, 20.